We All

~~Groan~~

Grown

A Teenager's Guide To Adulting

By Kim Posey Jones

Dedication:

To Keeley Shea Jones

Class of 2020

Go conquer the world!

I love you!

Table Of Contents

Author's Note

Groan (verb)—Make a low creaking or moaning sound when pressure or weight is applied.

Grown (past participle of grow)—Undergo natural development by increasing in size and changing physically; progress to maturity.

Isn't that what we are all doing? As high school seniors, your kids are groaning to get out, to be free from the oppression of the lower educational institutions. To move beyond the confines of teaching and embrace a paying job, or the romanticism of university life with its free thinking and superior intelligence.

As parents, we too are groaning. Groaning at every "last", every mention of graduation, every senior portrait, every cap and gown brochure, every college packet that comes in the mail. Groaning at the expense, the uncertainty, the prospect of our baby leaving home. Tears! Big tears. I don't want my baby to leave. I'm not ready. I don't think I will ever be ready.

She's grown.

I groan.

As her senior year progresses, rapidly I might add, it dawned on me that maybe I have failed her in some ways by not teaching her everything she needs to know before she graduates high school. Fear and anxiety press upon me that she might not be ready to fly the coop a year from now because of my neglect at teaching the basics. SO much to teach and so little time.

We All (Groan) is a fun, light-hearted attempt to cover some of the basics that everyone should know a little something about. It's not all-encompassing. It will not divulge the deep secret mysteries of life. Some of the things I write about, you will laugh at and wonder 'who doesn't know about this?' or 'how could anyone be so stupid?' But other things might just make you go, "Hmm…I never knew that." Either way, these are just some basics for you to ponder, meditate on, learn from, or disregard. The choice is yours. Your belief system may be different from mine. You may find that some of my tips don't work for you, or you have found a better way. Embrace it! I'm not right 100% of the time. What I do have is a few years of wisdom and a lot of failed attempts and regrettable mistakes. Hopefully you will garner a few pearls of wisdom.

With that said, neither my daughter, Keeley, for whom I am writing this book, nor her brother, Jeran, who will graduate five years after her, like to read. (Eye roll.) Shocking to me, as reading is mine and their dad's favorite hobby! Losing myself in a book is one of my most cherished pastimes. So, if the two of them read the preface I will be shocked! Though, hopefully, they will read further, learn more and actually enjoy it. I'll try to keep it light and short and entertaining.

Good luck to me!

Kids…keep reading! ☺

Part One

(Spirit, Mind

& Body)

Chapter One

Have a Daily Quiet Time

This is important on a soul level. I spend my quiet time propped up in my bed listening to worship music, reading my church devotional and daily Bible reading while drinking green tea with honey and lemon. It's a ritual that I love. It starts my day off right with the Creator of the Universe. Now, I work at night and sleep during the day, so when I say it starts my day off right, I mean at three or four o'clock in the afternoon. There is no wrong time to draw near to Him. He is always awake and eager to hear from you. So, find a time that works for your schedule and dive in. If I have extra time, I may watch a recorded sermon on TV (Joseph Prince is my favorite) and take notes.

The point is to get close to the Lord so that I can hear what He wants to say to me that day. I don't always hear from Him. I don't always obey what He is telling me. I don't always understand. I'm not always focused, but every day I get stronger, more knowledgeable, less like me and more like Him (I hope).

Make time every day to center yourself. Before you face your day, take a deep breath and acknowledge that there is a Higher Power, and give Him the first of your time to work wonders in your life. It is never wasted time.

Our best friends are on staff as pastors at a church about an hour away from us. It was his dream to be an international pastor one day. For years he held on to that dream. For as long as I have known them, they have each maintained a quiet time where they get alone with the Lord. I'm sure they were discouraged at times when nothing was taking shape like they wanted, when doors were closed. But they were sowing seed. It took years and years, some heartache and disappointments before the opportunity presented itself for them to step into, what was originally, his dream. Now they both serve, are both ordained to ministry, and are both international pastors. Because they were faithful to spend time with the Lord, He was faithful to give them the desires of their hearts (Psalm 37:4).

God is faithful!

Psalm 46:10

"Be still, and know that I am God; I will be exalted among the nations, I will be exalted in the earth."

Chapter Two

Speak Kindly to Yourself

Don't let your mind control who you are. Your mind will tell you that you are stupid, you are worthless, you will never amount to anything. You can believe those lies or you can wake up every day and speak what you want to see.

Like I mentioned previously, I work night shift and have for many years (well, all of my kids' lives). I feel like I have walked around like a zombie for most of their lives. The mantra I consistently spoke was how tired I was. Well guess what? Because I kept declaring how tired I was, I *was* always tired. When I heard a teaching about speaking what I wanted to see rather than what I saw, things changed. It wasn't overnight, but gradually I started waking up and saying things like, "Thank You, Lord, that I am well rested, that I am strong and energetic. This is the day the Lord has made. I will rejoice and be glad in it."

I changed the way I felt by changing what I said. I constantly say nice things out loud to myself. It sounds crazy and if other people were to hear me, they would think that I'm insane. I don't really care. Here are some examples of positive things to say to yourself:

I walk in divine health. I am healed and whole. (Sometimes my feet and knees hurt, sometimes my bulging disc flairs up)

I am happy and joyful. (Sometimes I am down in the dumps)

My debts are paid, and my bank account is full. (Sometimes our bank account is at $5 and we owe on our credit card)

I am blessed and favored. (Sometimes I wonder if this is true)

I am the disciple whom Jesus loves. (Sometimes I question why He would choose someone like me)

Today will be a great day. (Sometimes I don't necessarily feel this way)

I am smart and wise. (Sometimes I *really* have to step out in faith on this one)

I am kind and generous. (Sometimes I feel selfish)

I am the size and shape I am designed to be. (This is not what I see but what I want to see, remember??)

Those are just a few examples. Feel free to come up with your own nice things with which to affirm yourself. Or, take the promises in the Bible and declare them over yourself:

I am the head not the tail.

I am the righteousness of God in Christ.

The same Spirit that raised Jesus from the dead lives in me.

The angel of the Lord encamps around those who fear Him, and He delivers them.

There are so many promises and declarations that you can make over yourself. Seek them in His word and start changing the way you see yourself.

"Kind **words** are like honey – sweet to the soul and healthy for the body." –Proverbs 16:24

"A person's **words** can be life-giving water; **words** of true wisdom are as refreshing as a bubbling brook." –Proverbs 18:4

Chapter Three

Be Healthy/Stay Active

One of my biggest regrets is not staying active. In high school, I was an athlete. I was fit and muscular. In college, I continued to exercise and work out. By the time I was 22, I started drinking alcohol and going to clubs. Exercising and workouts weren't on the top of my priority list. I slowly started gaining weight. Fast-forward to marriage with two kids, a semi-sedentary life with a sporadic workout routine, and shiftwork, and I am now carrying around an extra 70 lbs. ☹

I enjoy walking. I actually enjoy working out. The elliptical machine is doable. However, making time for any of it is the question. Will I today, or won't I? My doctor friend recently told me, "You make time for the things that are important to you." Hmmm…most days, that thing is sleep. (Here is where I would insert a shrug emoji). Side note –

that's something I could invent, emojis for books. (Another shrug emoji).

My advice is to find several cardio and strength/firming workouts that you can mix up and do regularly. Skinny is not the goal, healthy is. You are beautiful just as you are, right where you are. If there is something you don't like about yourself, work to change it.

Trust me when I say it is easier to stay lean and fit than it is to lose extra weight. Especially when your back aches or your knees hurt or your joints squeak.

"Do you not know that your bodies are temples of the Holy Spirit, who is in you, whom you have received from God? You are not your own; you were bought at a price. Therefore, honor God with your bodies." –1 Corinthians 6:19-20

Chapter Four

Try New Things

Explore the world around you. Don't be afraid to order something different, try a new hobby, go with a radical haircut or color, or just take a chance on something new. Sometimes you will fail, sometimes you will be disappointed, but, every once in a while, you will be exhilarated and challenged. Life is not meant to be lived in the shadows or to always take the safe road. Sometimes you have to step out of your comfort zone to see what you are truly made of.

By all means, don't take this as a license to be reckless and to throw caution to the wind. Be safe and be smart, but take a risk every now and then to fall in love, dance like no one is watching, learn a new hobby, invent book emojis (wink wink), etc. We are creative beings made to explore and seek. Be a seeker. Seek truth, seek new things, seek friendship, seek success and accomplishments. Seek rest and peace. Seek a deeper relationship with Jesus. Live your best life!

Our Heavenly Father makes all things new.

"Behold, I am doing a new thing; now it springs forth, do you not perceive it? I will make a way in the wilderness and rivers in the desert." –Isaiah 43:19

Chapter Five

It's OK to Be Different

Contrary to the world's views, you don't have to be just like everyone else. It's OK to express yourself differently, view things differently and have an opinion that differs from those around you. Individuality should be celebrated, but we tend to criticize and make fun of those who are different than us.

Be the different person, or at least the person who accepts the people who are different. I can't say that I always embraced my differences while growing up, but there are a few things that I feel make me a little different:

I do not have a tattoo. I don't have a problem with tattoos. At one point in my life I wanted one, but never got around to it. **And** I have a low pain tolerance, so any mild discomfort is a big NO for me. (Eye roll) That makes me unique in that most people now have tattoos. I like being unique, even if it's something as small and insignificant as having or not having a tattoo.

I don't normally use cuss words and I don't particularly like movies or shows that use excessive cuss words. I'm not a prude and I have used cuss words in the past. In my 20's, I went wild and said and did just about anything and watched anything and everything. Now in my 40's, I don't see the need for it. At least not as it is overused in film. Sometimes I can see where a cuss word or two might be warranted, but the overkill of the foulest of words is unnecessary. Garbage in = garbage out.

I love Kenny G, Dave Koz, "Yacht Rock" and easy listening music. I have been a huge fan of Kenny G since my 20's. I think I have all of his CDs. I love his music and his talent, and I often get made fun of for my love of elevator music. Don't care! I enjoy the calmness and soothing sounds of his saxophone music. I thoroughly enjoy the Yacht Rock channel on SiriusXM, with its delightful old school easy listening sounds. I'm unapologetic about it.

I know that when you're in your 40's, it's totally different than being in your teens and 20's. Peer pressure is real. I get it. So, if you need to be a closet Kenny G lover, go ahead, but sometimes you just need to be okay with looking and sounding different from the world around you.

"Before I formed you in the womb I knew you, and before you were born I consecrated you;" –Jeremiah 1:5

Chapter Six

Be Open to Change

Life is a constant moving entity. Things change and things stay the same. Be open to that change. Sometimes change is going to happen whether you want it to or not, whether you're OK with it or not (Like your oldest child graduating high school). Learn to roll with the punches. It can be hard, I know, but for your own peace of mind, let things go that you cannot control. Learn to make the best out of every situation. That's not just sucking it up, it's learning to live a life in a world that always has and always will change.

Evaluate whether the issue will matter in five minutes, five days, five months or five years. If not, then don't treat it like it's the end of the world. Disappointments happen, but they are not the whole of your life, they are just a part.

Focus on the one constant that we have assurance of:

"Jesus Christ is the same yesterday, today and forever." –

Hebrews 13:8

The truth of Jesus is that He loves you, He is for you, He is

forgiving of you. Seek out the promises in the Bible that He

made thousands of years ago. They are still true today and

will be tomorrow.

Chapter Seven

Be a Student of Life

There are things to be learned every single day. Maybe it's the word of the day on a roll of toilet paper, or how to make coffee a different way, a new language, or a new route home. Our minds were created to learn. Don't think that because you are finished with high school and you are not going to college that you are done learning. Don't think that because you are going to college that that is the only place you can learn. Life is about learning.

Live with your eyes wide open and you will see the plethora of opportunities you have to expand your knowledge.

I remember way back when I was in ninth or tenth grade that a friend from elementary school moved back to our school. She was so smart…like, noticeably smart. She wore smart like Miley Cyrus wears leotards. I remember asking her how she was so smart, and she told me that she read all the time. And, almost 30 years later, I remember that. You can learn so much by reading, even if it's a sappy love story, a true crime novel or a work of fiction. Your brain sees sentence structure and punctuation and new words. The more you see them, the more you remember, and the smarter you become.

That same girl went on to be one of the valedictorians of our graduating class. She scored a 33 on her ACT, earned a degree in economics in college, then became a successful librarian, wife and mother. She became the Supervisor of Library Media and Fine Arts for Shelby County, Alabama and then received her doctorate – all while raising a family. She is now the Dean of Academics at a prestigious private school. To say she is smart is an understatement. She is still extremely smart but what stands out about her, other than the fact that she is kind and compassionate with a heart for Jesus and so very wise, she continues to seek knowledge. She gives real advice and is never condescending. She has gained many years of knowledge and continues to seek wisdom. She is a true student of life.

"I instruct you in the way of wisdom and lead you along straight paths." –Proverbs 4:11

Chapter Eight

Surround Yourself with the Right People

I've heard it said many times, "Show me your friends and I'll show you your future." That statement is so true. You will become like the people you surround yourself with. When I was in my 20's, I was dating a guy and ended up spending a lot of time with him and his friends. They went to clubs and bars and drank every night. At that time, I didn't drink alcohol and never had. But after months of feeling like the person on the outside, I gave in to the pack mentality and started drinking just so I would fit in with their crowd.

This is not a chapter on whether drinking is right or wrong, it's just my example of how you become like the people you are around. If you hang out with people who use drugs, eventually you will too. If you hang out with people who are always talking negative or have a bad attitude, you will too.

If you want to rise above, achieve more and become more, then surround yourself with people who lift you up, people who act and talk like you want to develop into. My best friend is the most positive and uplifting person I know. Her laugh is infectious, and her spirit is joyful. People are drawn to her because she is what people aspire to be; happy, kind, energetic, compassionate, encouraging. There has never been a time that I was around her that I wasn't encouraged and inspired.

That's the kind of people you need to have around you, people who lift you up and make you want to be a better version of yourself.

Your people define you. Your people are your lifeline. Your people are the ones that you can depend on, and that you know will drop everything to be there when you need them. I've mentioned already, or I will mention, some of the most important people in my life. Maybe not by name, but just a nod to the ones who I call my circle. They are the influencers, the cheerleaders, the prayer warriors, the constants in my life. Other than my mom, my kids and my husband, I don't talk to these people daily, but that doesn't matter much when your souls are knitted together. There is a bond that cannot be broken by time or distance.

"Become wise by walking with the wise; hang out with fools and watch your life fall to pieces." –Proverbs 13:20 (MSG)

Chapter Nine

Find an Adult Confidant

Everyone needs someone to talk to. Find someone – a parent, a relative, a teacher, an adviser, a pastor, a counselor – that you are comfortable with telling your innermost struggles. Everyone goes through hard times. Everyone has done something they wish they hadn't. Everyone could use some advice every now and then. It's OK to talk to your bestie about stuff, but sometimes you need wise counsel, and wisdom only comes from years of life experience.

Talking and expressing yourself can be tough at times. It can be embarrassing. Find someone who won't judge you, loves you unconditionally, and wants to see you succeed, someone who wants you to have the best possible outcome in all aspects of your life. Or, find a professional life coach or counselor that can help you navigate those pesky teenage years.

"Get all the advice and instruction you can, so you will be

wise the rest of your life." –Proverbs 19:20

Chapter Ten

Suicide Is Never the Answer

This is a heavy topic, but an important one. We all go through, have gone through, or will go through times when we are depressed, afraid and alone. Know that you are not alone! Everyone in your life may have abandoned you. You may feel worthless and unloved, but you were created for a purpose. The God of the Universe formed you and knit you together in your mother's womb. You were not an accident. There is a plan and a destiny for your life. You may have messed up really bad or gotten off track and you feel there is no way you can set yourself back on the right path. **That is a lie from the devil!** Your Heavenly Father adores you and forgives you and restores you. You can start over right where you are, all you have to do is ask Him.

In my 20's, I married young and divorced young. After the divorce, I felt like a failure and had to be temporarily put on antidepressants. The antidepressants helped me over the initial pain and shame. A few years later, I was in a long-term relationship with a man that I found out had been cheating on me the entire two years we dated. We had even talked about marriage. When I found out that his new girlfriend was pregnant, I lost it. I called him, crying and holding a gun in my hand. I wanted to die. He told me not to do it, then hung up.

It was a low point in my life and I'm pretty sure alcohol was involved in influencing my poor decisions. The only thing I could think of at that time was, "How will my mom, dad, sister and grandmother handle me killing myself?" Fortunately, my suicidal thoughts ended that night. But some people struggle daily with thoughts of self-harm. You have to know that the sun WILL shine again. It won't be easy, it may take a lot of time and therapy and prayer, but you are worthy!

Seek help! This world is better with you in it, despite the voice of the evil one that is telling you otherwise. John

10:10 says, "The thief comes only to steal, kill and destroy; I have come that they may have life, and have it to the full."

The enemy wants to destroy you by any means necessary. If you weren't an integral part of creation, he wouldn't try so hard to bring you to ruin. You are important, don't forget that! Your life matters! And this earthly life is only temporary; there are greater things in store if you just keep pressing on!

Chapter Eleven

Don't Ignore Your Sixth Sense

We all have one – a sixth sense. It's that funny feeling you get in the pit of your stomach, the hair on the back of your neck that stands up, that uncomfortable awareness that something isn't completely right. **Don't ignore it!**

If you're uncomfortable around a person or in a situation, LEAVE. Your perceptions and intuitions are usually a warning sign.

I was raised in the South where good manners and southern charm are taught from birth. I also have the personality of a peacemaker and I hate making people upset. It's difficult for someone like me, and maybe you too, to be rude or hurt someone's feelings. I remember as a kid, probably about 13 years old, going to the grocery store with my mom. There was a teenage boy who worked there who was probably eighteen or nineteen years old. Every time we went into the store and he was there, he would wink at me. I was so uncomfortable and scared, but never told my mom. I don't know why I didn't, but I never did. And his actions may have been innocent, but I knew that he was too old to be winking at a kid my age and it made me scared. I don't know whatever happened to that guy. He may be an upstanding citizen in the community, or he could be the local pedophile. I don't know. I do know that I should have told my mom about how I felt, how awkward it was for me to be in the same store with him, and that his behavior was not wanted or appropriate.

Intuition, or sixth sense, can be an argued subject, from the psychological perspective to the paranormal, but I believe that God instills in all of us a warning mechanism (Holy Spirit) that alerts us to trouble or danger. Be perceptive to your internal warnings – they just might save your life one day!

As of this writing, sex trafficking and juvenile abductions are on the rise. It seems like every day I read where someone has been taken or someone is missing.

Alcohol and drugs lower your inhibitions, meaning you are more likely to leave a bar with a stranger than if you had not been drinking. You are more willing to say yes to things you should say no to. Keep control of your faculties. Make smart, sober decisions and pay attention to your sixth sense.

Chapter Twelve

Take Care of Your Teeth

Once you get your permanent teeth, those are the ones you will have for life. Teeth can make or break you. Brush and floss at least twice a day and visit your dentist at least two times a year. (Smiley face)

Coffee and red wine and blueberries stain your teeth. After consuming these you should brush your teeth. Oreo cookies are a dentist's nightmare. Brush that yummy sweetness off as soon as possible. Dentists recommend brushing for two minutes. I do too!

While a pretty smile will give you confidence, the opposite is true also. An unattractive smile makes you self-conscious and timid. You may not have the resources to attain a perfect smile, but you can make sure to brush and floss and keep your teeth as healthy as they can be.

In addition to brushing and flossing, I use breath spray constantly. In truth, I am probably addicted, but I love to have fresh breath. And there is nothing wrong with having fresh breath. As a matter of fact, there is everything right about having fresh breath. So, there's that.

"A glad heart makes a cheerful face…" –Proverbs 15:13

Chapter Thirteen

Hygiene

Hygiene is very important. Good hygiene lowers the risk of sickness and disease. It makes you feel more confident and it cuts down on malodorous (unpleasant) smells. Essential hygiene rules are to bathe or shower daily, use deodorant/antiperspirant, wear clean clothes, and brush your teeth at least twice a day.

You should always wash your hands with soap after using the restroom and before and during cooking. If you sneeze or cough you should turn your head and sneeze or cough into your elbow or a handkerchief. If you are sick, you should wash your hands more frequently to avoid spreading your sickness.

You can use cologne or body spray to **add to** your clean smell, but don't overdo it! Those products will not cover bad hygiene! Keep your body clean, especially areas with a lot of sweat glands and where bacteria can grow.

Keep your nails trimmed and clean underneath.

Hair and face washing can be tricky. If you have dry hair, you may need to wash your hair every other day or every two days. If you have oily hair, you may need to wash it more often. If you have dandruff, you will need a special shampoo.

If your face is prone to breakouts, you will need to find a face wash and a cleaning regimen that works for your skin. Sometimes that takes years to figure out. And that in itself is so frustrating! I have been there and still in my upper forties have days when my face breaks out…UGH! If your acne refuses to go away, you may have to consult a dermatologist.

If your skin is dry, use a lotion or oil that you like. If your lips are dry find a lip balm that you like.

There is nothing that boosts self-confidence than to be freshly showered, neatly dressed and smelling good. Take pride in your cleanliness and in your appearance.

"Cleanliness is next to godliness" –John Wesley

Chapter Fourteen

Integrity

Integrity (noun)—The quality of being honest and having strong moral principles.

That's the dictionary definition of *integrity*, but I think of integrity as doing the right thing even when no one is watching.

Where to begin with this one.

Being honest seems like a no-brainer. Having moral principles seems like a basic trait that all humans should possess. And I guess they all do but just forget to use them. Or rather, choose not to use them.

Be the person that people can count on, the person that people can trust to do the right thing. My husband is that person. He is honest to a fault. I never question his motives or the way he handles his business because he is a man of integrity. He lives above reproach in his work life and in his personal life. He is a hard worker with a servant's heart. He always does the right thing. Be that kind of person.

While we're on the topic of doing the right thing; people matter. Treat people the way that you want to be treated. That is a simple rule. It is what's known as the Golden Rule. Live by it.

Treat people with kindness.

Realize that everyone has struggles. Everyone has things they are dealing with and going through. Everyone has hurts and everyone has bad days. A little grace for other people will go a long way. You never know when you might need the same thing.

"Do to others as you would have them do to you." –Luke 6:31

Chapter Fifteen

Work Hard

"There are few things more satisfying than doing a hard day's work." –Me

Now, someone before me may have thought this or actually coined it, but I couldn't find where anyone has said this and made it a thing. So, here I go being a trendsetter…coining phrases and such.

Regardless of who said it, it is satisfying to work hard, whether at your job, in your yard, in your house or on a project. Sometimes sweat is therapeutic. Hard work is gratifying even if it's just unto yourself. You may or may not get praised for what you have accomplished, but nevertheless, the end result of your hard work is rewarding, whether it's a clean house, a fresh yard or a completed task.

Always do your best.

The Bible says in Colossians 3:23, "Whatever you do, work at it with all your heart, as working for the Lord, and not for man."

Be deliberate. Be focused. Be the example. Build your character and endurance. Notice I'm talking about the tasks you take on, to do with excellence – not working longer or more hours.

Have a reputation as a hard worker, a loyal employee, a faithful laborer, a dependable teammate and friend. My sister is that kind of person. She works harder at her job than anyone else I know. She labors hard to do every part of her job with excellence so that her clients are completely satisfied.

Chapter Sixteen

Don't Procrastinate

As a parent there are few things more annoying than when your kids procrastinate something that you have told them to do! (Angry face) It has been said that delayed obedience is really disobedience. I totally agree! There are times when you can't immediately do something you are tasked to do, but the majority of the time you can.

SO, DO IT!

For Pete's sake, DO IT!

For the sake of your mother, DO IT!

Procrastination is such a stressor. I hate putting things off, even things I don't want to do. I would just assume suck it up and do it and be done with it. This goes for schoolwork, your job, or chores your parents assign you. Just do them when you are told to do them, and you will not be stressed out and your parents will not have to nag you and your boss will not have to ride you.

Know that you are not the only one feeling stressed out over your assignment. If your boss gives you something to do, don't delay, don't wait, just get it done. Your boss is feeling stress waiting on you to complete your task. Your parents are stressed waiting on you to finish your chore(s). Your teacher is probably not feeling stress because they can give you a bad grade and go on about life.

Just a little side note, parents HATE nagging you and constantly having to fuss at you! It's exhausting and draining and makes us feel bad. Then you feel bad or guilty and no one is happy. (Sad face) And all of these negative emotions could have been easily avoided if you just did what you were told from the start!

As far as school assignments go, start working on them when they are assigned. If it's a research paper, start getting organized and do a little research each day instead of waiting until the week it is due. You will be glad you did. No

one ever regretted starting and/or finishing an assignment
early.

Not procrastinating also applies to obedience to what
the Lord instructs you to do. He only wants what is best for
you, so you would be wise to obey and not procrastinate.

"I will hasten and not delay to obey your commands." –
Psalm 119:60

Chapter Seventeen

Guard Your Heart

I don't really know what to say about this other than what it says; guard your heart. Be selective on who you give yourself to. Don't shy away from relationships for fear of getting hurt but proceed with caution. Matters of the heart are tricky and exhilarating and fun, but they can also be painful and unhealthy.

You are worthy and should be treated as such. Don't let anyone put you down, demean you or abuse you (mentally or physically). There are places you can go and resources to help you get out of a harmful relationship.

Let's get to the basics of love – because too many people stay in abusive relationships because they are "in love".

What is love?

1 Corinthians 13:4-8 says, "Love is patient, love is kind. It does not envy, it does not boast, it is not proud. It does not dishonor others, it is not self-seeking, it is not easily angered, it keeps no record of wrongs. Love does not delight in evil but rejoices with the truth. It always protects, always trusts, always hopes, always perseveres. Love never fails."

That's pretty clear cut.

I admit in my younger years, I didn't guard my heart. I gave away pieces of myself to everyone I dated. So, when I finally met "Mr. Right" (my husband), I was damaged goods with issues and baggage that had to be healed over time. I regret that for his sake. He deserved far better than I brought to the table.

So, for your future spouse, guard your heart! You don't have to fall in love with everyone you date. Date and have fun, date in groups instead of alone, but **don't sleep with everyone you date.** Definitely do not feel pressured to have sex.

This leads me to our next topic, and it's a hot one…

Chapter Eighteen

Let's Talk About Sex

This chapter is going to be long.

Sex is a highly debated topic. As a parent, I want my kids to wait until they are married before they have sex. As a once-upon-a-time teenager, I know how difficult that can be. And the truth is, parents cannot control when and if you have sex (Spoiler, I know). Especially if you have a car and are not under house arrest. And the pressure you guys face is much greater than I had in the late 1980's to early 1990's.

Sex is everywhere – movies, TV, music, in your schools. There really is no escaping the impact that sex has on our culture and specifically your generation. Sex is accepted as a given if you are in a relationship for any amount of time. It is almost expected, and most definitely assumed. Let me encourage you to wait. Waiting will be difficult and will for sure go against the culture, but it will be well worth it.

Pastor Chris Hodges from Church of the Highlands preached a fantastic 5-part series from the Song of Solomon. I encourage you to watch or listen to it. It is incredibly insightful about how our bodies were designed to go forward into sex once the kissing and petting starts. It's extremely hard to stop that forward momentum once it gets going, so avoid getting to that point.

Sex is a special unity between a man and woman in marriage. It is a gift from God and, like most things that are good and pure and holy, Satan has perverted it. I'm going to leave this right here because I know there are many who will disagree, argue and accuse me of not being open-minded or inclusive. That's not the case at all. I'm simply giving my beliefs based on what the Bible teaches. You are free to believe what you believe and know that I'm not judging you for your choices.

Moving forward…

If you find yourself in a position where you have crossed a line or have gone further than you had planned,

ALWAYS USE PROTECTION! This is not a word of advice; this is mandatory for your life. Not even once should you ever have sex without using protection. No exceptions!

One of my dearest friends from elementary school is a doctor at a clinic near a popular university. Every time we get together, she emphasizes the importance of talking to our kids about sex and using protection because of the number of STDs that she sees daily. The majority of cases are from young adults who were planning on waiting until they were married to have sex, but things went too far and here they are with a disease that they will carry with them for the rest of their life. These are good kids. Having sex before marriage doesn't make you a bad person. It doesn't make you unlovable or too far from the will of God.

You can't look at someone and assume that they do not have an STD just because they look clean. It's a risk you do not want to take! Some diseases are not only annoyingly uncomfortable or permanent, but deadly. Love yourself enough to protect your body. Don't put yourself in situations where you will be tempted to do something you are not comfortable doing. Have a plan. And I'm sorry to say, abstinence is not the only plan. Have a backup plan.

STDs aren't the only risk here. An unwanted pregnancy will lead to even bigger life decisions and choices you may not be ready to make. There is so much responsibility in creating a life. The decision to be sexually active in your teens is a heavy burden that you place on yourself. So don't!

Think of sex like a giant present that is under the tree on Christmas morning. It is wrapped up beautifully and has your name on it. The expectation and excitement when you wake up and it's time to open your present is beyond comparison. But, what if before that present was wrapped you found it in your parent's closet and secretly had been taking it out and using it for weeks while your parents were away? Would you be as excited about this present on Christmas morning? Probably not. Don't rob yourself of one of God's greatest gifts. It will, without a doubt, be worth the wait.

When I was young, I had always planned on waiting until I got married before I had sex. That is a great idea, in theory, but how was I going to do that? When I decided that I would wait, I didn't have a boyfriend. That makes waiting so much easier. But when I was sixteen, I started dating a guy. And at sixteen I thought I was in love. Before long we were having sex. That wasn't my plan. That wasn't what I wanted to happen, but I put myself in situations where we were alone, and I allowed the kissing to go on to a point where I couldn't have stopped if I wanted to.

Again, I stress to date in groups. Love life as a teenager. It's some of the best times of your life. You will create wonderful memories during this time. Don't be so serious and 'in love' and confined to being around your boyfriend/girlfriend all the time. If you are living your best life with friends having innocent fun, you will have no regrets when you get older. Trust me on this! There is plenty of time for serious, grown-up, heavy duty love. But with that comes a lot of responsibility. A responsibility that most teenagers are not mature enough to handle. Don't put that stress on yourself. And just for the record, statistics shows that about 2% of high school sweethearts end up getting married, so…

Bottom line, abstain, and if not, **ALWAYS USE PROTECTION!**

Let me add a little bit to this.

NO PDA! NO ONE, ESPECIALLY YOUR PARENTS, WANT TO WATCH YOU MAKE OUT WITH YOUR SIGNIFICANT OTHER! For the sake of your parent's eyeballs, don't subject them to that. (Or they just might give it back to you!) That doesn't mean go to someplace quiet to be alone-that's danger! Respect each other enough to not compromise. Respect your parents and their parents.

Chapter Nineteen

Drugs

DON'T DO IT! JUST SAY NO!

I'm not using these cute little catch phrases to be blasé or trite. I mean it when I say DON'T try drugs! Not once, not ever! It's like playing Russian roulette; your chances of survival are very low.

In this day and age drugs are everywhere. Honestly, drugs scare me. Drugs make me sad when I think about how many lives are destroyed daily by drug abuse. It's so easy to laugh at a drug addict and think "how pathetic" or "that will never be me" but the truth is, no one ever tries drugs thinking, hoping or expecting to become a hopeless, homeless addict that can't kick the habit. For years I watched the show *Intervention*. You see the addict and then you see their family, be it kids or parents. As a watcher of the show, it seems absurd that a mom would choose to get high instead of choosing her kids. But at some point, the addict no longer chooses. Their need for the high is stronger than their love for their family.

Medicalnewstoday.com defines *addiction* as "a psychological and physical inability to stop consuming a chemical, drug, activity, or substance, even though it is causing psychological and physical harm." The addict has given his/her body something that it will now crave and desire more than anything else. Willpower and self-control alone can't free you from the clutches of a drug addiction. Some people can say that they would cut the user off, or they would let them rot…that their problems are their own fault. But I have always pondered, "What if that were my child?" There is nothing I wouldn't do to save one of my kids. What a hopeless situation it is when you love someone so much that you will lose everything to save someone who doesn't even know that they need to be saved. Or maybe even want to be saved.

I firmly believe that one of the devil's greatest schemes is drugs. It starts out simple and harmless. Just a way to dull the pain or ease the hurt. It's just something that you do for fun or for recreational use or because everyone else is doing it, or because you've had a serious accident and then can't get off the pain meds.

The case for marijuana being or not being a gateway drug is a long-argued discussion. I've known people who tried marijuana when they were young and never tried anything else. I've also known people who tried marijuana and went on to harder, more addictive drugs. So, whether or not marijuana is a gateway drug is not the issue. The underlying issue, in my opinion, is what is your reason for wanting to try any mood-altering or psychotropic or highly addictive drug or narcotic? A captain at the police department where I work once said (loose paraphrase) that not everyone who tries marijuana goes on to harder drugs, but every person who uses hard drugs started out smoking marijuana. Again, that is a very loose paraphrase because I couldn't find the actual article where he was quoted. But that makes a lot of sense. Argue for or against marijuana being a gateway drug, but that is neither here nor there. If it's just to have fun, find another way! It's not worth the risk! If there is another, more destructive reason behind your need to cover or mask your pain, seek counseling or help. Again, drugs are just not worth it!

A pastor friend of mine says, "Sin will take you farther than you ever wanted to go and keep you there longer than you ever wanted to stay." That's exactly what drugs will do to you and for you. It's a trap, a trick, a farce. Don't be fooled. Your life literally could depend on it!

I can't imagine the pressure your generation is under to succumb to peer pressure and social media image. When I was in my party phase in my 20's, I was already divorced and felt worthless and like a loser on so many levels. I had failed. I had made bad choices. That kind of led me to not caring much about doing the right thing or making the right decisions. I had a trail of bad judgments following behind me. However, by the grace of God, I landed a police dispatch job which subjected me to random drug tests. I don't know if I would have tried drugs had I not been hired by this agency, but I am thankful that drugs were never a temptation because I knew I could and would be tested. Even when I wasn't spiritually sound and on solid ground, I had a higher calling that kept me from choosing drugs; a career that I loved and wanted to excel in. I had a purpose. That's what a lot of people are missing; a purpose. Proverbs 29:18 says, "Where there is no vision, the people cast off restraint (or the people perish)…"

You were created for a purpose! Find your purpose! Everyone has one. Everyone was made for something. Don't discount yourself because you've made mistakes. Pick yourself up and reach your destiny!

Chapter Twenty

Drugs Part Two: Addiction and Other Important Issues

After writing the last section, I felt I needed to add some things about the *why* of drug abuse and addiction. I mentioned before that I used to watch the show *Intervention*. I am not a doctor, a therapist or an expert in drugs, and I didn't stay at a Holiday Inn last night. Let me clarify that now. I don't know the chemical components of drugs or how or why they affect people. I am someone who notices things, well, sometimes I notice things. What I noticed most about the show is that the majority of people addicted to drugs or alcohol had been raped or molested at some point in their life.

THIS BREAKS MY HEART AND ENRAGES ME!

That kind of abuse should never happen to a person. Ever! And it makes me understand why they would want to mask their pain and/or shame. It's a hurt that I can't even begin to comprehend. It's a violation that is so perverse and inhumane that it physically makes me ill. I cry for people that I don't even know because of a hurt that is so inconceivable.

If you happen to be a victim of such crimes, talk to an adult, a teacher, a pastor, a counselor. You are not to blame. You are a victim that can become a victor with the right guidance. You don't have to carry this burden alone. Don't try to self-medicate. That will only end in disaster. In one of Tyler Perry's Madea movies, Madea says something along the lines of "hurts that are covered up don't heal." That is very true. You can't keep covering up pain with stuff; be it drugs, alcohol, gambling, shopping, sex. Whatever it is, you need to deal with the issue. It takes a strong person to get down deep into the root of the problem, to find out what is causing you pain and to resolve it.

YOU ARE THAT STRONG PERSON! I BELIEVE IN YOU! BETTER YET, GOD BELIEVES IN YOU!

While we are talking about don'ts…don't try cigarettes or vaping. Both are addictive and contain harmful chemicals. If you never try it, you'll never be addicted. And it will save you a ton of money! (Thumbs up emoji)

Chapter Twenty-One

Take Responsibility for Your Actions

Too often in this day and age people are quick to blame others. We blame others for our problems, our failures, our bad fortune, our bad choices. We're quick to blame God for not protecting us, or for allowing bad things to happen. We blame our parents or grandparents for the things they did or didn't do while raising us. The truth is, we are responsible for our choices and our actions. Like in a previous chapter, if you have unprotected sex with someone who has a venereal disease and you contract that disease, who is to blame? YOU!

You are responsible for you. No one else is.

If you charge too much on a credit card and can't pay it back, it's not the credit card company's fault that you are in debt because they gave you credit. It's not the waiter's fault that you ate too much at the restaurant, nor is it the bartender's fault that you drank too much.

We need to start owning our mistakes and failures and **learn from them.**

Chapter Twenty-Two

Marriage

Don't take marriage lightly. Marriage is a sacred commitment between two people. A covenant. An oath. In biblical times, you would *cut* a covenant, meaning blood would be shed. It was, and still should be, a solemn vow unto death.

Today it is so easy to get a divorce and walk away from a lifeless marriage. It's easier to part ways and things than to fix what is broken. We are a fast-food, instant gratification, "me" society. We see the greener grass and think that is what we really want, when in reality, were we to obtain that, it would be just as dissatisfying as our current situation.

When my husband and I got married, we decided then that divorce was not an option. We staked our marriage on it. Come hell or high water, we were in this together and we would do whatever it took to make this last. Since we both came from broken homes, we knew that we didn't want our kids to have to go through that. It was a commitment that we made then and, almost 20 years later, it is still stands. We are committed to the commitment.

There is total security in knowing that someone has pledged an oath, and means it, to stay with you until death. Choose wisely.

"Therefore a man shall leave his father and his mother and hold fast to his wife, and they shall become one flesh." – Genesis 2:24

Chapter Twenty-Three

Take a Sabbath Rest

For years, I ran on all cylinders. I felt like I had to be constantly moving, doing, and accomplishing in order to be effective in life. It took many years of being tired and weary for me to finally relent and give in to the fact that God created us to work six days and to take a day of rest once a week. I read a good book about taking a Sabbath rest and it really resonated with me. Since then, I have purposefully tried to act on this and do all chores on the other days and leave one whole day to do absolutely nothing. This right here is my wheelhouse. Not to brag or anything, but I excel at taking a Sabbath. There are few things that I love more than being in my PJ's, sitting in my bed reading and napping. If Sabbath was a spirit animal it would be mine.

If we are not going out to eat, I try to have an easy crockpot meal prepared. I try to have the dishwasher unloaded beforehand so that all dishes can go in and I don't have to wash them on my day of rest.

You don't have to be religious to take one day a week to rest. Your rest doesn't have to look like mine or anyone else's. I like to go to church on Sunday morning, eat lunch then come home, put on my PJ's and crawl into bed for an undetermined, unplanned amount of time. I usually read until I'm sleepy, then take a nap. It could last an hour or 3 hours…who knows? It's nap roulette. That's the beauty of it!

My husband likes to read out on the back porch while smoking a pipe. My kids like to nap or play on the computer. To each his own on Sabbath rest!

Once I wake up, I love to veg out on the couch and watch TV or sit on the back porch with my husband and listen to music and just talk. I love when my kids want to hang out with us or watch a show together.

I love those days when I can do this. I am relaxed and focused and ready to go into a new week when I take time to do what I enjoy. Sabbath doesn't have to be Sunday. Sunday is my day because it's the only time I can step away from responsibilities and claim a rest. For my husband, he has to work on Sunday, so he takes a Sabbath on Tuesday. I'm usually asleep, the kids are at school, so he can enjoy his day without interruption and obligations (usually). Your Sabbath just needs to be a day when you don't have to work, when you can unplug and disconnect so you can recharge your battery.

"Then He said to them, 'The Sabbath was made for man, not man for the Sabbath.'" –Mark 2:27

So far, we have covered the basics of the spirit, mind and body. Now let's get to the practical parts of life. The things that everyone should know a little something about. Everyday common sense that often isn't very common.

Part Two

(Practical)

Chapter Twenty-Four

College Isn't for Everyone

This may rub some people the wrong way. I am all for achieving your best, for striving for your goals, and for being the very best version of yourself. But, with that said, I will reiterate my opening statement, COLLEGE ISN'T FOR EVERYONE! Some of the smartest people in the world didn't go to college, or didn't finish college: Bill Gates, Steve Jobs, Mark Zuckerberg, to name a few. Now, these above average intelligence entrepreneurs may be the exceptions to the rule, but the point is made. However, there are some jobs that require a college degree. If you have decided that one of them is what you want to be, then college is a must. Like doctor, lawyer, nurse, engineer, teacher, accountant, etc. You all, please go to college! (Thumbs up)

However, going to college just to go to college or to find out what you want to be or because everyone in your family went, or because no one in your family went is not economically wise. Always seek knowledge and education, but some people learn better with hands-on experience. Education is not limited to a classroom at a university. College should be a great experience of learning, growing, and exploring your new-found independence. So, let's take a quick look at exploring economics.

Johnny wants to be a police officer. The average salary for police officers nationwide in 2016 was around $62,760. College tuition can run anywhere from $10,000-$40,000/year depending on in-state or out-of-state to community college, etc. So, let's say that Johnny goes to college at $35,000/year X 4 years = $140,000. When Johnny graduates, he owes $140,000 right off the bat for his education (assuming he wasn't loaded and paid cash but had to take out student loans). If Johnny moves out of his parents' home and lives on his own, or even with roommates, and if he gets the job he wants right out of college, it will take a long time for Johnny to pay off his loan.

I don't say all of this to discourage you. If you have your heart set on going to college, or if your parents insist that you go to college, go! My advice is not necessarily for the college-bound, but rather the students on the fence about college, the students who feel pressured to go to college even if they aren't the best students, or those whose career choices don't require a degree. There should be no shame for choosing a career path over a college degree, or for taking a year or two off after high school to explore what you want to be in life. It's hard to know exactly what you want to do with the rest of your life at sixteen, seventeen or eighteen years old.

I will make a few exceptions. If you are a talented athlete, musician or a Brainiac and can get a full ride scholarship to college, you would be remiss to pass up that opportunity.

Another regret that I have is that I went to college right after high school even though my heart was not fully in it. I was 'in love' and that was where my attention was. I dropped out and got married only to divorce two years later. Then, I started back part-time at a junior college while I worked a full-time job **and** a part-time job. After I got my job as a 911 dispatcher, I enrolled at a university and finished my degree in criminal justice about eight years after I graduated high school. (I could've been a doctor! HA!)

The part I regret is not being fully involved in college. I didn't get to know people and I didn't go to games or functions because I always had to work. I wish that I had truly experienced the college life. But you live and learn and hopefully pass on these nuggets to a younger generation.

Other post-high school options are trade schools, technical schools and vocational schools. There is nothing wrong in learning a trade or a craft. Plumbers, mechanics, electricians, heavy equipment operators, to name a few, are noble professions that are often in demand and pay really well. Skilled laborers are a necessity in everyday life. Mark Twain said, "Find a job you enjoy doing, and you will never have to work a day in your life." That's a true statement!

Another option is missions. One of our dearest friends is a missionary in Honduras and has been for several years. During her senior year of high school, we all went on a mission trip together. She felt called to return as a teacher. Years later, she married a wonderful Honduran man with a heart for the Lord and they are living and serving the community that she has grown to love. And she is now expecting her first child! And the best part about it – she did not incur a huge college debt **and** she is now fluent in Spanish!

"Wisdom is more precious than rubies; nothing you desire can compare with her." –**Proverbs 3:15**

"Jesus grew in wisdom and in stature and in favor with God and all the people." –**Luke 2:52**

Education, knowledge and wisdom are extremely important to have. The way you go about getting them is up to you and how you are hardwired. Don't think less of yourself if college is not for you or is not for you *right now*. The most important thing you can do is follow God's leading and direction. Don't force yourself into a box that doesn't fit you. But if you know what you are called to do and college is a part of that, don't hesitate.

One of my oldest and dearest friends graduated high school, went to college, got her B.S. in Early Childhood Education and Elementary Education (double major!) and became a teacher. Five years later got her Master's degree in Elementary Education and then a Master's degree in Education Leadership. She knew that was what she wanted to be. She excelled as a teacher, became a vice principal and, this past year, became the principal of an elementary school in the city where we grew up. She continued her education and sought higher learning for a greater purpose. She pours herself into her students, faculty, teachers and staff. To me she embodies Luke 2:52.

Chapter Twenty-Five

Keep a Hard Copy Calendar

Everyone has a phone nowadays with a calendar on it. Technology is awesome and useful, but you should always have a backup. When it comes to calendars, I am old school. I carry a two-year calendar in my purse, and I have a one to two-year calendar hanging on the kitchen wall. No one in my house really looks at the calendar except me. But I feel that the calendar keeps our lives from going off the rails. I am constantly updating them with practices, doctor appointments, games, meetings, work schedules, etc.

A written calendar is a great alternative to your phone calendar in case you lose your phone or there is some malfunction. In addition to the redundancy, I keep calendars from each year. It's a great way to document life milestones and significant events. In years to come, when I'm old, I can look back on them and remember some moments that were special or some mundane tasks that I performed.

When my grandmother passed away a few years ago, we found old calendars and address books with funny quotes and sayings that she had written in them. It was a bittersweet reminder of how fleeting life is. But it was also a moment to laugh at how funny she was, how witty her sense of humor was. You can't get that on a cell phone.

By nature, I am not a very organized person. I am more of a free spirit, a spontaneous soul, but some things require a more precise timeline. Anything that starts at a certain time or has a specific agenda necessitates punctuality and management.

So, have a backup calendar that you can look back on and smile at some of the things you've done.

"But all things should be done decently and in order." –1 Corinthians 14:40

Chapter Twenty-Six

Grammar

This will not be a complete grammar lesson but a few of my pet peeves:

There, their, they're

Your, you're

Its, it's

Affect, effect

Me, I

Seen, saw

There is a location or place.

Their refers to something owned by a group.

They're is a contraction for 'they are'.

Your is possessive (you own something).

You're is a contraction for 'you are'.

Its is possessive.

It's is a contraction for 'it is'.

Affect is a verb (that affects me).

Effect is a noun (that had a great effect on me).

Me and I

People, even educated people, get this wrong most of the time. If you are saying *Jerry and I are going to the store* that is correct. But if you say *Can you take Jerry and I to the store?* that is incorrect. Rule of thumb: Take out the other person in the sentence and see how it sounds. Can you take *I* to the store? NO! Not only can you not take I to the store, but that is incorrect grammar usage. People think they sound proper by using 'and I' but oftentimes it is not correct.

Saw is the past tense of the verb 'see' (I saw you from across the room).

Seen is the past participle of the verb 'see'. *Seen* requires a helping verb. Past participles **cannot** appear by themselves.

I have seen that before.

I had already seen that before today.

You're welcome! (Not, your welcome!) ☺

Chapter Twenty-Seven

Learn to Pack

This one seems so absurd. It seems simple enough, and if you're a dude it's even simpler. Packing takes practice. My daughter can pack for herself, but she does better if I make her a packing list. I make myself a packing list as well, and I make one for my son (even though I still pack for him). It depends on how long you will be gone and where you are going, but here is a sample packing list for a three-day soccer tournament, as a spectator, during the summer:

2 PJ's	Toiletries
Sweatshirt	Fan
Sleep socks	Charger
3 sports bras/undies	Book
Black tank top	Water bottle
Black shorts	Chair

Blue tank top

Multi-colored shorts

Pink tank top

Gray shorts

3 socks

Tennis shoes

Black yoga jacket

Tent

Cooler

Bug spray

Sunscreen

This is just a quick list to give you an example of how I usually do the packing. If we are taking a long vacation, obviously the list is longer and much more detailed. But by doing it this way I seldom forget anything. Plus, marking off a list gives me a sense of accomplishment. Don't judge. I make lists for all kinds of things just so I can mark them off after I do/buy/pack them. It's the little things.

Chapter Twenty-Eight

Learn How to Balance a Checkbook

This seems like common sense, but balancing a checkbook is not something that is often taught in school. You should know up front how much the monthly fees are for your bank for a checking account and a savings account. (It's never too early to start saving!) The basics of keeping a checkbook is to start with a deposit. Banks usually require at least $25.00 to open an account. Today, your work can direct deposit your paycheck into your bank account (super convenient), or if you don't have a job, your parents can deposit or transfer money into your account (super spoiled). A check register has lines where you can write deductions and deposits. If you have a savings account, it can be linked to your checking account as an overdraft protection (more on that later). Each blank line in your register will have a place

for a check number, the date, the transaction description
withdrawal amount, deposit amount and balance.

EXAMPLE

DATE	TRANSACTION	PAYMENT	DEPOSIT	BALANCE
01/01	paycheck		1000.00	1000.00
01/02	tithe	100.00		900.00
01/02	to savings	90.00		810.00
01/03	gas	25.00		785.00
01/04	food	68.45		716.55
01/06	movie	30.00		686.55
01/06	movie snacks	20.00		666.55
01/07	oil change	28.35		638.20
01/08	gift fr grandma		200.00	838.20
01/09	tuition	450.00		388.20
01/09	books	150.00		238.20
01/10	bank fee	5.00		233.20

This is just a quick example of how to keep a
checkbook. It's not complicated, but it is necessary to be
accurate so that you don't withdraw more than you have.

Overdrawn accounts can lead to fees approximately $35.00 per transaction. *Overdrawn* simply means you have spent, written checks or taken out more money than you had originally put in. This is where that savings account can come in handy. But be advised that each time you overdraw from your checking account, the bank will take the amount out of your savings to cover the lack, but they will also charge you a fee. So, stay on top of your money and live within your means, even if that requires not going out when everyone else is or not buying those shoes you want. Don't spend all you make. Control your money, don't let your money control you!

Chapter Twenty-Nine

How to Write a Check

Check writing is almost obsolete in today's world, but there are still a few occasions where you may need to write a check. Most people use their debit cards or pay with cash, and the majority of people pay bills online, so writing a check is not as common as it used to be. However, just for argument's sake, let's go over the basic way to write a check. The lines are labeled and are pretty much self-explanatory.

Fill in the date line: June 28, 2019 or 06/28/2019 (either way is acceptable).

Pay to the order of _________________________ (write to whom you are making out the check). Example: John Doe

Write the dollar amount in the amount field: Example $343.52

The long line under the "Pay to the order of" line and the $ amount box is for you to write the amount out in words. Example: Three hundred forty-three dollars and 52/100---------

The "for" line is optional but can be a reminder to yourself why you paid this person or company. If you are paying a bill, this is where you put your account number.

The bottom line on the right-hand side of the check is where you sign your legal name in cursive.

And that's the nuts and bolts of writing a check. Make sure you write in your ledger the check number, the date, to whom and the amount!

Chapter Thirty

Tithing/Saving

I am a strong proponent of tithing. A tithe is ten percent. I believe if you give God the first, He will bless the rest. With that said, let's do some basic math. (This is also shown in the checkbook example in the last section.) Let's say you make:

$1000.00

-10% (100.00)   tithe

$900.00

-10% (90.00)   savings

$810.00   expenses/bills/entertainment

This discipline will teach you how to live on 81% of your earnings while saving and honoring God with your finances. If you can adopt this practice at an early age, you will have control over your money.

If you don't see a need to give God the first, that is up to you. But I highly recommend it.

When our daughter was young we started teaching her about tithing on everything she made. She puts 15% aside for tithe and offering and 15% into the savings. It has now become an automatic for her. She is forming life skills that will benefit her for the rest of her life and is showing that she is willing to submit her money to a Higher Authority.

"Bring the whole tithe into the storehouse, that there may be food in my house. Test me in this," says the LORD Almighty, "and see if I will not throw open the floodgates of heaven and pour out so much blessing that there will not be room enough to store it." –Malachi 3:10

Chapter Thirty-One

Credit Cards

While we're talking about money and finances, let's talk about credit. Now, most people will argue this point as to whether or not to get a credit card. By the time you graduate high school, creditors will have you in their sights – fresh meat. There is nothing more exciting than seeing that credit card offer arrive in the mail with your name on it. You are officially a (groan) grown up when you can apply for and receive your very own credit card.

You think the sky is the limit and all your worries are over. If you run short this month, just charge it; if you want those shoes, charge it; if everyone is going to the beach for the weekend, just charge it.

PUMP THE BRAKES!

A lot of people, and I mean *a lot of people* get into trouble by running up charges on a credit card that they believe they will be able to pay off when they get that good job, or that better job. According to lexingtonlaw.com, in December 2017 Americans owed $834 billion in credit card debt alone. 43% of Americans spend more than they make each month and rely on credit cards to make up the shortfall. Do not become part of this statistic! Debt is no joke. Debt is a burden, a stressor that weighs on you for years and years. Don't assume that you will have that dream job after college and all your money troubles will disappear. The fact is, it may take years and many menial jobs before you land that good paying job. Don't set yourself up for failure. Learn now, even before you get a credit card, to live on less than you make, and save, save, save!

I was once an idiot, especially with finances. Occasionally, I still am. In college, I got the obligatory credit card applications and applied for a couple. Those companies smelled naiveté and inexperience from a mile away. They were all too happy to say yes to this ignorant nineteen-year-old kid. I kept my debt low, a couple of thousand, nothing too extreme. Then I got married and divorced, bought a mobile home, worked full time at an insurance company by day and at a local Walmart three nights a week while going to junior college two nights a week to try and finish my degree (in what, I had no idea).

At twenty-two, I met a guy and we started dating. He lived in a townhouse and I got a friend to agree to move into the apartments in his complex. I sold the mobile home and moved into my first apartment. I quit my insurance job and my Walmart job and started working part time on commission at a fitness center. (Shrug, eye roll, smacking my head) That's when credit cards became a way of life.

My roommate and I took short trips to New Orleans and Atlanta every other weekend. We charged groceries and hosted parties and bought fabulous clothes to go out dancing in, which we did three and four nights a week. How did we manage to pay our bar tabs?? You guessed it, those same credit cards. I got a good paying dispatch job working for a local police and fire department. And, after two years of dating this one guy, we broke up. I managed to buy a house and lease a car and continue with school and work, but by the time it was all said and done, I owed $20,000 in credit card debt. My job, although good paying, couldn't pay for a house, a car, my bills, life and debt. Not my finest hour. (tear drop)

By 1999, I met my husband and knew instantly that he was "the one." We talked about my debt, as it would affect him if our relationship continued. With no other option, I was forced to file bankruptcy on my credit cards. That was a hard pill to swallow, a blow to the old ego…another failure to add to my list of failures.

After years of rebuilding, I have managed to acquire an 800+ credit score, something I am very proud of. It's been a long, hard road, but my husband is financially savvy and has taught me many things about saving, spending and managing credit cards. After 19+ years of marriage, I'm still learning.

Credit cards and small loans are important to establish credit, but you have to be responsible and **only charge what you can afford to pay for**. If you have the cash for that TV or those shoes, **charge it, then pay it off.** Keep doing that month after month and you will have built up your credit. A good credit rating makes buying a house or a car or any other large purchase you want to make in the future much easier.

So, stay out of debt, build up your credit score, honor God with your money, save for a rainy day (because everyone has one), and your future self will thank you!

If you need further information about money, debt and credit the Bible is loaded with verses to guide you in making good decisions regarding these topics. There are also financial advisors that can give you practical money advice.

"The rich rules over the poor, and the borrower is the slave to the lender." –Proverbs 22:7

"Owe no one anything, except to love each other, for the one who loves another has fulfilled the law." –Romans 13:8

Chapter Thirty-Two

Tipping

This is a biggie if you have ever been a waiter or waitress. Most people don't tip like they should. Mainly because no one teaches you how much to tip, when to tip and why.

The food industry is something almost everyone takes part in. Some more than others. Eater.com gives a few hard rules when it comes to tipping. At a sit-down restaurant 20% is the standard. For delivery, 20% is good and $5 is the minimum. Food trucks and bakeries and delis $1-$2. If the gratuity is already included in your bill there is no need to add an extra tip.

Almost everyone has a cell phone with a calculator on it. Figuring a tip amount is just a few buttons away. If your bill is $85.62, put in your calculator 85.62 + 20 % ($17.12) = $102.74 or $102.75. Easy.

Why tip? Most waiters and waitresses are getting paid as low as $2.13/hour, far below the average minimum wage of $7.25. That's not a lot of money, so they depend on your tips to survive.

Not all waiters are created equal. Some seem to have been born for the job while others are just trying to get by. Whatever their reason for waiting tables, it's a hard, often thankless job. I challenge you to be a good tipper even if your service isn't stellar. You never know what someone is going through or what kind of day they are having. Treat others like you would like to be treated – after all, that is the Golden Rule!

*Guys – trust me when I tell you that a girl will notice a guy who shows respect to the wait staff by being a generous tipper.

"And as you wish that others would do to you, do so to them." –Luke 6:31

Chapter Thirty-Three

Taxes

America has one of the most complicated tax systems in the world. I could end here…

But I'll trudge through this hot topic for the sake of you, my young reader. Let me clarify, I am not an expert. I am not an accountant. Truth be told, the IRS is probably looking for me. (Just kidding…I hope!)

Taxes are hard to understand. They are frustrating, sometimes unfair, often too much. Once you begin a job, your employer will start taking out taxes from your paycheck based on your state, your filing status, dependents and other factors. Taxes are taken out of your check and put in the Federal Reserve. On April 15th, everyone is required to file their taxes and they will either pay the shortage or receive a refund check for their overpayment.

That's the simple version. Find an accountant if you need further explanation because I can't help you.

Sales tax is another way that we the people are taxed. When you make a purchase, you will notice that taxes are added to your total amount. The city and state where your purchase is made will determine what percent your taxes will be. There are state and local taxes, which can be alone or combined, depending on your area.

It often feels like we are taxed to death. And the real question is what is the local, state and federal government doing with our money? Are they managing it in a positive way? Or are they mismanaging those funds and lining their own pockets?

"Then Jesus told them, 'Give to Caesar what is Caesar's, and to God what is God's.' And they marveled at Him." –Mark 12:17

Now I'll give you directions in doing math.

Just kidding! (laughing emoji)

Chapter Thirty-Four

Get Out and Vote

Now, I hate politics. And for the most part I distrust all politicians. With that said, I vote. Because I am free to vote. Because women before me fought so that I would have the right. Because I want a voice in who gets into office. Because my vote matters. Because I get a sticker.

OK, maybe not the last one. Although I do feel like I've done my civic duty. One thing you should do is study the candidates and align yourself with the candidate that shares your beliefs and convictions. Don't vote one way just because 'Daddy always did'. Vote your conscious, vote the way that will make this country a better place.

Try to see the candidate aside from the mud slung on him/her by the opposing candidate. Be aware of the political climate, the social issues and the pressing matters that are being talked about. Learn enough about our government and our history to have an educated discussion or debate.

I fail miserably at this.

So, do better than me.

Chapter Thirty-Five

Read a Map

Like a real, fold-out, paper, color-coded, map-keyed map.

I know you've seen one before. They're those strange disposable rectangular objects, that are akin to a complex origami creation that you can never refold the right way in your parent's glove compartment. (A glove compartment is that not-so-secret alcove in the dash on the passenger side front seat of a vehicle).

Phones have spoiled us with built-in GPS and someone to walk us directly to a location. But if you lose your phone or there is no cell service, you could be in big trouble without a map.

We have taken many soccer trips over the years. More often than not, a soccer field or soccer complex is strategically hidden in the far depths of a pasture (hence the shoddy cell service) or in an inconspicuous neighborhood. Many times, we have "arrived" at our destination only to be in front of some random person's house with no goal in sight. I learned very quickly to have a printed copy of directions and a printed map with me for all travels.

Now, on to actually reading a map:

Make sure you have it where you are reading it in the right perspective.

Find the compass that is usually in a corner. North will always be the top of the map.

Familiarize yourself with the map key or legend which shows important symbols and what they mean.

A map scale will show you how far places are on a map. For example, 1 inch = 20 miles.

Figure out where you are on the map and where you want to go. You can make two circles on your map and draw a line between them.

Use the map scale to determine roughly how far you will need to go. Your path may not be a straight line, but this will give you an idea.

Follow your path, being aware of your surroundings.

When my daughter first started driving with me in the car, I would ask her where she was periodically. I wanted her to know what interstate she was on; what direction she was traveling. I wanted her to see things around her so that in the event of an emergency she could get help quickly.

Recently, my family and I drove across the country in an effort to see the Grand Canyon and other iconic sights along the way. My husband bought an atlas (a book of maps). Our atlas had a map of the United States, then a map of each individual state. My husband plotted a course using said atlas. We didn't make plans other than to start out westbound on one route and, after reaching the California coast, to turn around and come back a different way. It was so liberating and fun and spontaneous, and so not planned.

Chapter Thirty-Six

Pumping Gas/Putting Air In a Tire

The other day, a woman in her early 20's asked my mom to help her pump gas. My first thought was that she had a partner and they were trying to run a scam on her (that's the downside of working for a police department). The woman was not running a scam, she just had never been taught how to pump gas. (Stunned face)

Learning to pump gas and how to put air in a tire should be taught when you are learning to drive. Sometimes when you know how to do something you just assume that everyone else knows how to do it as well.

SAFETY FIRST at the gas pumps! Don't ever smoke around a gas pump (don't ever smoke anyway – see Chapter Twenty). Don't talk on your cell phone. Turn off your car engine. Any kind of static electricity can cause a spark which can cause a fire.

The first thing to do is to turn your car off. You can either pay at the pump with a credit/debit card or pay with cash inside the store. If you pay with cash inside ALWAYS lock your car. A lot of criminals are opportunistic, just waiting for an easy score. Don't make it easy for them. If you pay at the pump, be aware of your surroundings. I was told by a bank employee once to always select 'credit' even if you're using a debit card. If you choose 'debit' the retailer blocks off $50-$100 to authorize the purchase. By using 'credit' the gas station does not put a hold on your account for $50-$100, just the amount you spend. Choosing credit can also make you less vulnerable to identity theft.

Once you have prepaid for your gas, remove the nozzle from the pump and place it in your tank. Select the octane level you want to use: Regular grade (about 87), Mid-grade (about 89) and Premium (91-93). Obviously the lower the grade, the cheaper the gas. Do not use the pump that says "diesel" (it's usually green) unless you are driving a diesel engine vehicle (if you're driving one, you'll know). Some pumps have you lift the arm from where you removed the nozzle, while others don't. If your pump has an arm, lift it. Next, you will squeeze the handle on the nozzle and gas will be dispensed into your tank. Some pumps have a lock on the handle so the gas pumps on its own until the tank is full, while others do not, and you have to hold it down until the desired amount of gas is in the tank.

When you have finished pumping gas, lower the arm on the pump, remove the nozzle from your tank and place it back on the pump. Take your receipt from the machine and close your gas cap. Do not drive off with the pump still in your gas tank! (It happens more often than you would think.)

Putting air in your tire is not difficult. On the inside of most driver's side doors is a chart of recommended PSI for your front and rear tires. PSI stands for 'pounds per square inch' and is the common unit of measurement for pressure. Most gas stations have an air pump. Pull your vehicle up to the pump, insert coins if the pump requires that you pay for air, remove the cap off the stem sticking out of your tire, place the hose on the stem and a bar will stick out showing you a number which tells you your current PSI. You will need to press the lever on the hose to dispense air into your tire. If your tire PSI is too much, just place the hose on the stem and air from the tire will escape. Either fill the tire or deflate the tire until the correct PSI is achieved.

While we are talking about cars, here are a few helpful hints:

Make sure you get your oil changed as often as recommended by your mechanic. This will extend the life of your car and improve gas mileage by removing particles and sludge.

Keep your gas tank at least half full at all times. This will come in handy in the event you get lost or there is an emergency.

Keep the inside clean and free from trash and wash the outside regularly. This will give you a sense of pride in your vehicle and make your surroundings more appealing for passengers. And, it helps maintain and protect your vehicle's appearance, thereby increasing your resale value.

I can't walk you step-by-step in this book on how to change a tire, but you should find a friend or mechanic that is willing to teach you. Each car is different, so there is no "one way" of doing it. Basically, you have to loosen the lug nuts, find the jack and position it correctly and jack your car up near the tire that needs changing. Then you have to use the tire iron to remove the lug nuts from the center of the tire. Next, remove the tire from the car, put the spare tire on, replace the lug nuts, making sure they are tight. Lower the car back down, tighten the lug nuts and then remove the jack. Again, get proper training on how to do this for your specific vehicle.

While you're learning how to change a tire, learn how to check your oil and add windshield wiper fluid. Most vehicles have a sensor that comes on the dash when your oil is low, but it's good to know how to do these basic things to maintain your vehicle.

Chapter Thirty-Seven

How to Wash Clothes

This is simple. My 13-year-old son can do it. Washing clothes. It's easy to learn and a necessity in life unless you want to depend on someone else to do it for you. The first thing you do is sort your clothes by color. Make a pile for whites only, darks and colors. Important note here, **REDS ARE DANGER**!! Wash anything red separate from everything that is not red, unless of course you want pinks, because that is what you will get if you wash red clothes with other clothes. And we did this just the other day (sad face).

My washing machine is old and sturdy, and I refuse to get a new one. I have a large capacity machine that may not be eco-friendly, but my clothes get clean and I like it! That's my choice. Machines will vary, but the premise is the same. You measure out the amount of detergent you need based on the size of your load. I generally wash large loads because that

is eco-friendly as opposed to washing in small or medium-sized loads (I do my part). You can use powder or liquid, whichever you prefer.

Measure your detergent and pour into the machine, turn your dial (if your machine has a dial) to the length of time you want to wash. I usually do 14 minutes, large load. Once my detergent is in and the water is flowing, I add my clothes that have already been separated into piles to the machine. Close the lid.

When the wash, rinse and spin cycles have finished, the machine will turn itself off. Then it is time for the next phase of washing clothes.

To dry or not to dry, that is the question?

Most cottons, linens and silks will shrink in the dryer, while polyesters, spandex and nylons won't. If you're not sure of the material, check the label inside the clothing and it will tell you. T-shirts and sweatshirts will shrink, so either buy them too big or **hang them up to dry**!

When in doubt, hang it up.

Put the clothes you want to dry inside the dryer, add a fabric sheet. Close the door, clean out the lint trap, set the level of heat and amount of drying time then press start.

Once your dryer has finished drying your clothes, you are ready to fold or hang them up, depending on your preference and/or space. I recommend hanging up clothes immediately out of the dryer over ironing. I hate ironing! If you hang your clothes up as soon as the drying cycle is finished, your clothes are less wrinkled. I hate to find a basket of clothes that have been washed and dried and are sitting in a basket for several days. It's one big basket of wrinkle.

Some clothes don't matter; PJ's, workout clothes, undergarments, socks. Who cares if they're wrinkled? But *my* work clothes!! Ugh!

A quick fix is to put a few articles in the dryer with a damp washcloth and re-dry them for 15-20 minutes. That should take care of the unsightly wrinkles. Or, you could set up your ironing board, plug in your iron to the setting of the type of clothes you need to iron, and iron the wrinkles out.

That's my last resort, but you do you.

Chapter Thirty-Eight

Basic Phone Rules

- Answer when your parents call.

- Use a hands-free device while driving.

- **NEVER text and drive.**

- Keep your phone charged.

- Don't *sext* (I mean really people, come on!!).

- For Pete's sake, don't take or send risqué pictures of yourself or anyone else (again, really??? Smacking my head). More on this later.

- Don't use your phone at the table.

- Don't watch anything that you wouldn't be comfortable watching in front of your mom.

- Phones are a privilege, not a right.

- Use good manners on the phone. For example: greet the person calling, don't just hang up when you are finished, end the call properly with a 'goodbye' or a 'talk to you later'.

There are severe repercussions for sending and receiving risqué pictures over your phone or computer, ESPECIALLY if you or the other party are minors.

Risqué (adjective)—Slightly indecent and liable to shock, especially by being sexually suggestive.

Example:

Let's say Mary is fifteen years old. She takes a topless selfie and sends it to her boyfriend, Joe. Joe is now in possession of child pornography. Joe passes it on to his friend Dave, and now Dave has child porn on his phone too. Dave sends it to Kathy because Kathy hates Mary and he thinks she will get a good laugh. Kathy uploads it to the whole school or posts it on social media to try to embarrass Mary. Mary should be embarrassed that she made a huge lapse in judgment and took that kind of picture AND sent it to her boyfriend. But all are guilty, and **ALL** can be charged

with a crime.

Chapter Thirty-Nine

Spend Time with Parents/Grandparents

Your relationship with your parents and grandparents will likely determine whether or not this section applies to you. Older generations are wiser and have stories and sayings and memories that are priceless. After my parents divorced, my mom, sister and I moved in with my grandparents. That experience taught me so much and gave me the opportunity to grow closer to my grandmother. My last living grandparent passed away two years ago, my grandmother on my mother's side. I was closer to her than my other grandparents, by far, and I enjoyed hearing stories from her teenage years, from working in a sausage factory, to meeting my grandfather.

I learned how to cook, mainly from her.

She was kind. She loved completely. She was funny and witty. She was smart.

And just like that, she was gone. And with her she took her knowledge and her experiences.

I miss that. I regret not making more time to visit with her.

I miss her.

As a parent, I can say that we love when you want to spend time with us! We love when you ask us for advice. We love when you are interested in the things we do and our opinion of things.

Becoming a parent has made me realize how important I am to my own parents. As my daughter prepares to graduate high school, the thought of her moving out makes me want to curl up in a ball and cry big tears. That's my baby girl and no matter how old she gets she always will be. There will never come a time when I don't want my kids around. And seeing that from a parental perspective hopefully makes me a better daughter.

Being able to call my mom every day is a gift that I hope I never take for granted. Realize that parents and grandparents won't live forever. There will come a day when they will pass on. Make time for them. Take in their wisdom, feed on their knowledge. Enjoy their stories.

You won't regret it!

Chapter Forty

Learn to Cook

Even if it's just the basics. Follow the package directions or the recipe.

Wash your hands before, during and after cooking, especially if you are using raw eggs, raw meat and raw chicken. Use a wooden cutting board for fruits and vegetables only. Use a glass or non-porous cutting board for raw meat. Don't use the same knife to cut raw chicken then use it to cut your vegetables.

Boiling water:

- Put a lid on it (this makes the water heat up faster).

- Depending on what you are boiling the water for, add a little butter and salt to keep it from sticking.

- Follow the directions on the packaging for boiling noodles or rice.

- Place eggs in a pot and cover with *cool* water to bring to a boil (keeps the eggs from cracking when you put them in the pot).

- Place a wooden spoon across the top of the pot to keep the water from boiling over.

Baking cookies, cakes or brownies:

- Baking dessert is precise, so you need to measure and follow the recipe EXACTLY.

- Make sure you have all your ingredients before you start.

Baking casseroles or some other dishes gives you a little more leeway to experiment and add to or leave out some ingredients. Baking simply means the bottom burner in the oven is the one heating or cooking your food.

Broiling in the oven uses the top burner and is used for toasting breads or browning the top of food or melting cheese, etc. Broiling only takes a few minutes, so you have to watch closely.

Watch the cooking channels for ideas, tips and recipes. Cooking can be a lot of fun. Knowing how to cook different things will add variety to your eating.

Clean as you go. Wash dishes or rinse and place in dishwasher as you finish using them. This will make cleanup much faster and easier. It will also make cooking more enjoyable. When washing dishes, use a clean rag, antibacterial dishwashing detergent and use hot water. Rinse thoroughly and place in a dish drain to dry, or hand dry with a clean towel.

Chapter Forty-One

Insurance/Benefits

When looking for a job, take into consideration the benefits and insurance that is offered. Some jobs may pay okay, but offer great incentives and benefits, like 401K, retirement, health insurance, life insurance, etc. In your late teens and early 20's, this may not be something that you even look at, but as you go further into your career, these things will be very important.

I started at my job as a public safety dispatcher when I was twenty-four years old. For the most part, I was ignorant about benefits and insurance. The pay was very good for not having a college degree (at the time I was hired I had not yet finished college). I focused solely on the amount of money I was making and didn't take advantage of all the perks that were offered. We have a deferred compensation plan that is basically a savings account you can put money into before the money is taxed. I just started that a couple of years ago. (Eye roll). I did know that, because it was a municipality, I had a twenty-five-year retirement. Most people and most jobs require that you work until you are sixty-five. Because I started my job at a fairly young age, I can retire with full benefits when I am forty-nine years old. That's crazy! I have less than two years until I can retire. That's a huge thing.

Insurance.

When I was single, my job paid 100% of my health insurance. That's a big deal. When I got married, I added my husband and then eventually my kids to my insurance plan at a fair rate.

My job also lets you accrue "off" time – sick time, vacation time and personal time – depending on your years of service.

So, my advice is to find a job or career that you enjoy doing, but that also has benefits that fit your needs and desires.

Chapter Forty-Two

Job Interview

(can also apply to meeting parents)

It is extremely important that you know how to interview for a job. The basics:

- Shower/avoid perfume or cologne.

- Dress nice.

- Be on time.

- Shake the interviewer's hand.

- Look them in the eye.

- Be energetic/positive.

- Have good posture.

- Use proper English (no slang) and speak clearly.

- Know a little bit about the job you are applying for.

- Sell yourself; talk yourself up; promote yourself.

- Have a copy of your resume with you.

- Be ready to tell a little bit about yourself; your interests, hobbies and likes.

- Thank the interviewer for his/her time and consideration.

Chapter Forty-Three

Don't Leave Drinks Unattended

Whether you are at a party or a bar, don't walk away from your drink and leave it unattended. The majority of the time, leaving your drink on a table or bar while you use the facilities or step away for a minute will be okay, but there are predators in the world that seek opportunities to spike or drug your drink for nefarious reasons. Don't take that chance, especially with people that you don't know very well. If at all possible, take your drink with you or have a trusted friend keep an eye on it. One of the worst things that can happen is to wake up in a strange place with no memory of what you have done or what has happened to you.

This is not just about alcoholic beverages; this is any drink. Use caution! Use good common sense. Pay attention to people who are paying too much attention to you.

In addition to this topic, DON'T EVER DRINK

AND DRIVE! DON'T GET IN A CAR WITH

SOMEONE WHO IS UNDER THE INFLUENCE!

DON'T LET YOUR FRIENDS DRINK AND DRIVE!

NEVER!

NOT ONCE!

NOT EVER!

Chapter Forty-Four

Learn Some Basic Fix-Its

I am notorious for trying almost any home repair, much to the dismay of my husband. Over the years I have installed a dishwasher, an over the stove microwave, and ceiling fans, to name a few.

Simple things like screwing a screw in:

Righty-tighty

Lefty-loosey

Nails hold better if you nail into a stud (usually a 2x4 board behind your sheetrock…not your hot neighbor). Screws secure better than nails.

Change a lightbulb: righty-tighty/lefty-loosey applies here too, and to most things that you twist to insert or remove.

WD-40 will make any squeak go away.

Don't fool with electricity unless you are sure you know what you are doing. Electrical shock is no joke! **Always turn the power off at the box** if you are attempting any electrical fix-it.

Some things can be fixed by loosening or tightening the screw.

Leaky faucets and running toilets may require a plumber, but you can attempt to tighten or replace small parts. The number one thing you need to remember is **ALWAYS TURN THE WATER OFF FIRST!**

Online videos can assist you in simple do it yourself projects.

Chapter Forty-Five

Your Path May look Different from Everyone Else's

So, college preview days are upon us. With that comes added stress and pressure. My daughter has no idea what she wants to do, where she wants to go, or what she wants to be when she grows up. And that's OK!

When she was four years old, we started her in soccer. This is her thirteenth year of playing. She spent many years loving the sport, wanting to play in college and maybe even professionally. Then a couple of years ago, she decided that she didn't want to play anymore, that she strongly disliked soccer altogether. (shrug) Since it's her senior year, we convinced her to play one more season. She is still not loving it like she once did. We see posts and updates almost daily where some of the girls she started out playing with have committed to playing soccer in college. It makes me happy

for the girls we have watched grow up follow their dreams

and make life-changing commitments. I could easily be sad

that my daughter has chosen to go a different route. I could

lament the thousands and thousands of dollars we've spent,

the hours we've practiced, and the miles and miles traveled in

the name of soccer. But I am not sad at all!

We thought we had a plan to take her to college. We

thought soccer was our only way. It turns out her interests

and priorities have changed. Such is life. An old Yiddish

proverb says, "Man plans, and God laughs." That is so true.

We could be upset. We could yell and tell her she is making a

huge mistake. We could insist that she play soccer to get a

scholarship to go to college. And I know some parents do

that. Some parents force their will on their children. But I

trust that my daughter is following her heart and seeking

God's will and His plan for her life. By the world's standards

it may seem that she is making a mistake, but I believe the

scriptures, "For I know the plans I have for you, declares the

Lord, plans to prosper you and not to harm you, plans to give you hope and a future."

What we have to remember most is that this life is temporary. The things of earth will pass away, but the Word of God will never pass away. (Matthew 24:35)

Don't conform to what everyone else is doing. Be you. Make decisions that the Lord leads you to make. Dress like you, walk like you, talk like you. Be YOU! You are fearfully and wonderfully made just like you are. The world would be a terribly boring place if we all acted and looked and sounded the exact same. Dare to be bold and make your own choices, following the gentle leading of the Holy Spirit.

Chapter Forty-Six

Wrapping It Up

There are so many other hacks, pieces of advice and words of wisdom that I could include in this book that it could go on and on forever. But to ensure that I haven't lost my audience, I'll end on this. Learn how to cut grass, write a letter, and take a self-defense class. Always wear your seatbelt. Always wear clean underwear. Be a good person. Learn basic coping skills, how to talk to people and resolve conflict. Practice making doctor's appointments or refilling a prescription. Learn how to dress for your body style and body type. Be comfortable learning about you and who you are and what makes you uniquely you. After all, growing is changing, maturing and developing. Dance to the beat of your own drum. Be fantastically, wonderfully you! There is no one else like you!

Don't lament lost opportunities or past mistakes. Every day is a new day full of new adventures, new opportunities and do-overs. If you fail, pick yourself up, dust yourself off and try again.

In the words of Henry Ford, "Failure is simply the opportunity to begin again, this time more intelligently."

So never stop beginning.

You are worthy, you are mighty, you are loved, you are cherished, you are awesome, you can be and do whatever you put your mind to. Aim for the stars, be the best version of yourself that you can be. Live life to the full, but always know that this life is not the final destination, it's just a layover; a brief stopping point on the way to eternity.

"Life is a gift, and it offers us the privilege, opportunity, and responsibility to give something back by becoming more." – Tony Robbins

BECOME MORE!

Acknowledgements:

When I began thinking about the acknowledgement page I thought it would be a simple thank the kids and husband and editor. But as I pondered more on the topic I realized that I have a lifetime of people to thank. God has truly blessed me with a circle of family and friends that are magnificent and irreplaceable. So, I give Him all praise for inspiration and for "my people."

First I want to thank my parents, Barbara Siener and George Posey for loving and supporting me through it all. You both gave me a foundation to build on and a lifetime of love and encouragement.

To my sister, editor, and friend, Shea Posey, thanks for making this book look great and making sure that my typos and grammatical errors weren't seen by the general public.

To Kristina Bergvall, who took one of my favorite photos and made it into a phenomenal book cover. I can't thank you enough.

To "Pop", my father-in-law, Jerry Jones, Sr. for always praying, loving and supporting us so well.

To our best friends, Matt and Holly Hobson who constantly pray for us, encourage us, meet us for dinner, vacation with us and love us. Your friendship and spiritual guidance is priceless.

To my "old school" friends, Heather Mays (the Dean of Academics), Michelle Brakefield (the Principal), and Nikki Christensen (the Doctor). Thank you for the dinners, the wisdom, the talks, the laughs, and the constant that you three are and always have been in my life. I'm so amazed that you three Enneagram 1's love and accept this 9 (at least that's what ya'll tell me I am).

To Shannon Coker, my college roommate, friend and co-conspirator in many shenanigans. A lot of the topics in this book were inspired by our reckless mistakes. We have come a long way.

And finally to Jerry, Keeley and Jeran. You three complete me! I don't know what I did to deserve you. Thank you for tolerating my lack of sleep and my crazy schedule. I love you!